WELCOME TO THE WORLD OF CONSTRUCTION VEHICLES!

Discover with us the amazing vehicles that build roads, bridges, tunnels, and much more! Embark on an exciting adventure with bulldozers, excavators, trucks, and many other powerful machines. **Get ready to explore every corner of the construction site and learn how these incredible machines work up close!**

DOWNLOAD THE BONUS
HERE ARE YOUR SPECIAL CONTENTS

a gift for you

Yes, that's right! We have prepared it just for you.
Getting the special contents is easy.
Follow these steps:

Visit the website: Open your browser and go to the page

> **Go to the last page of the book**

Enter the Code:
You will find a field where you can enter the following exclusive code:

> **Go to the last page of the book**

This code has been created especially for the book owners and will give you access to a bonus with unique resources that you can download directly to your device.

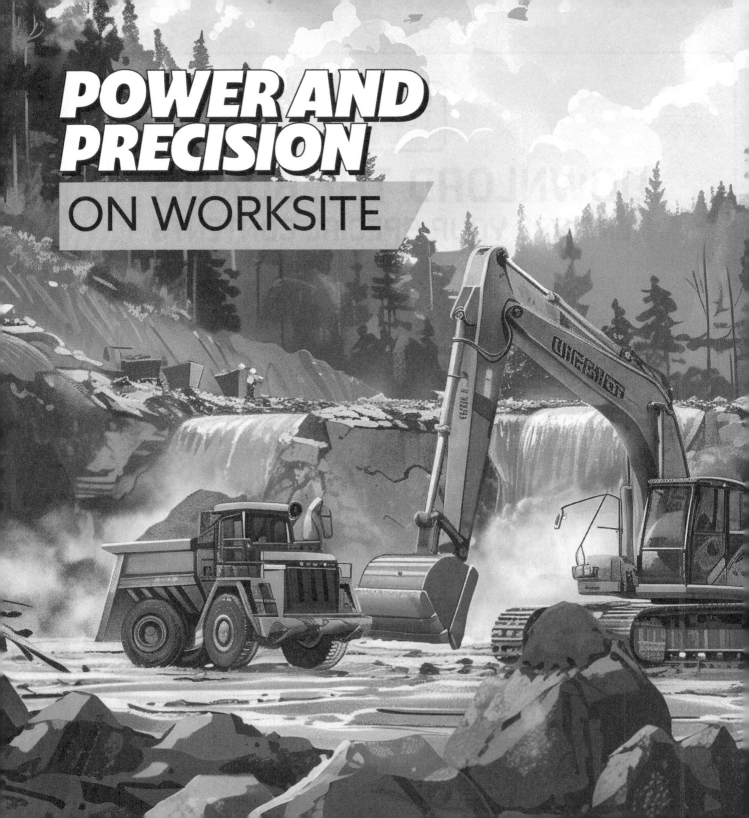

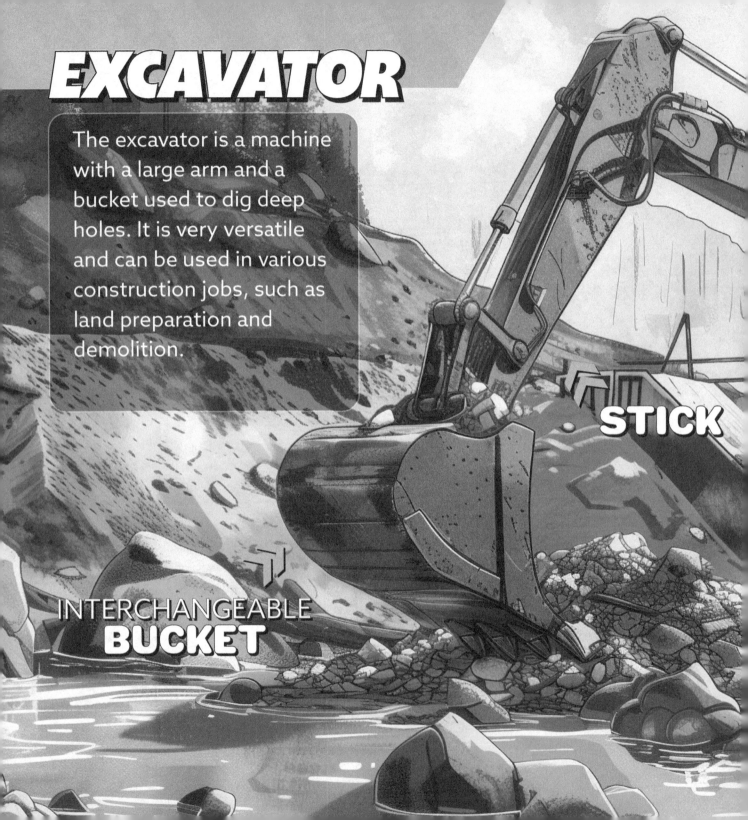

EXCAVATOR

The excavator is a machine with a large arm and a bucket used to dig deep holes. It is very versatile and can be used in various construction jobs, such as land preparation and demolition.

STICK

INTERCHANGEABLE BUCKET

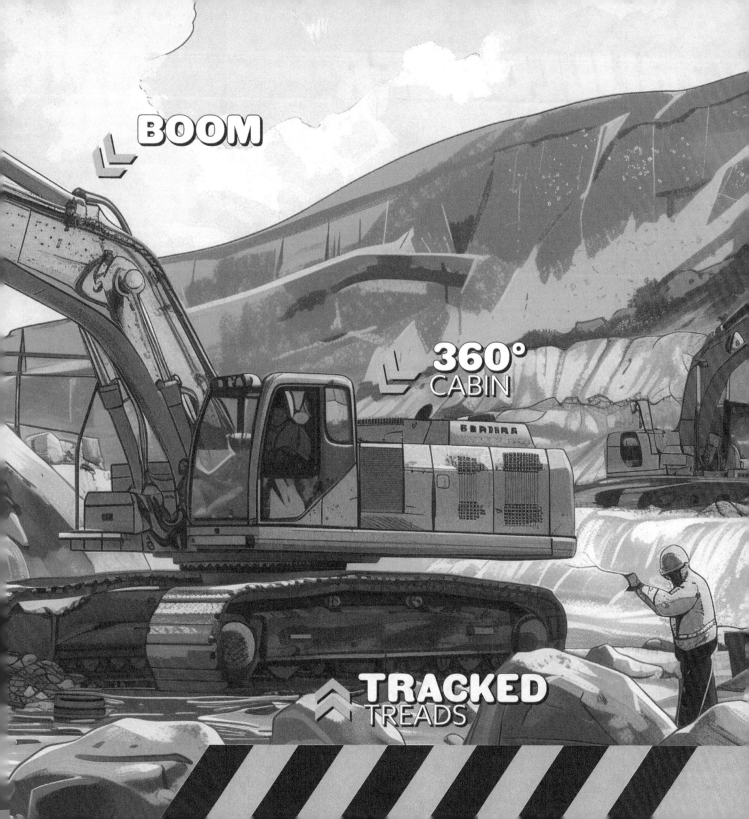

BULLDOZER

The bulldozer is a powerful vehicle with a large front blade to push soil and debris. It is used on construction sites to prepare the ground, level surfaces, and remove heavy obstacles.

The dump truck is a truck that can tilt its bed to unload materials such as sand, gravel, and soil. It is widely used on construction sites for the quick and efficient transport of heavy materials.

DUMP TRUCK

BUCKET »

MECHANICAL SHOVEL

The mechanical shovel is a vehicle used to dig and load materials such as soil and sand. With its large front bucket, it can easily move large quantities of materials on construction sites. It has sturdy wheels that allow it to move over rough terrain and perform the work with precision and efficiency.

DID YOU KNOW?

Can excavators have different types of buckets?
Yes! They can have buckets of various sizes and shapes to fit different kinds of jobs.

Can dump trucks unload materials in different ways?
Yes! Some dump trucks have beds that tilt backward to unload, while others can tilt sideways. This makes them very versatile for different types of work.

Can excavators work underwater?
Yes! Some special excavators are designed to operate underwater and can clean riverbeds and lakes..

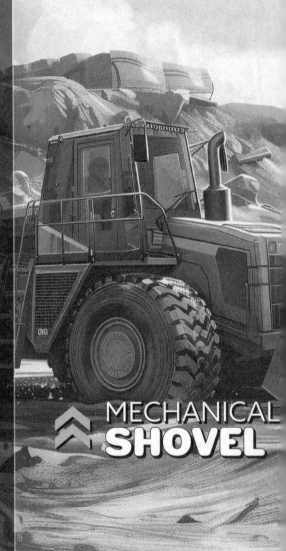

MECHANICAL
SHOVEL

DUMP
TRUCK

EXCAVATOR
WITH ARM

TANKER TRUCK

The tanker truck carries liquids such as water and fuel. It is essential on construction sites to provide vital resources, ensuring that operations can continue without interruption.

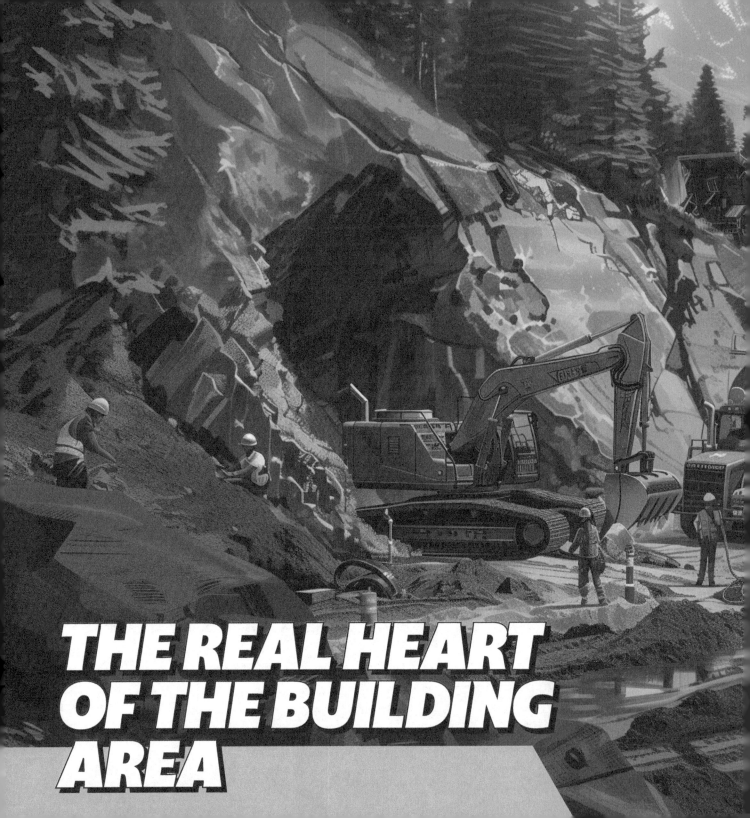

THE REAL HEART OF THE BUILDING AREA

The tanker is probably one of the most important vehicles on a construction site, especially in remote areas like forests.
Without the tanker providing fuel, other vehicles like bulldozers, excavators, and dump trucks couldn't work.
The tanker moves around the site, refueling every machine and ensuring that work can continue without interruptions.
It is the heart of the site, allowing all other vehicles to operate efficiently.

WORKING IN THE QUARRY

TRACKED BULLDOZER

The tracked bulldozer has tracks instead of wheels, making it ideal for difficult terrain. It is used to level, dig, and move large amounts of soil, especially on uneven surfaces.

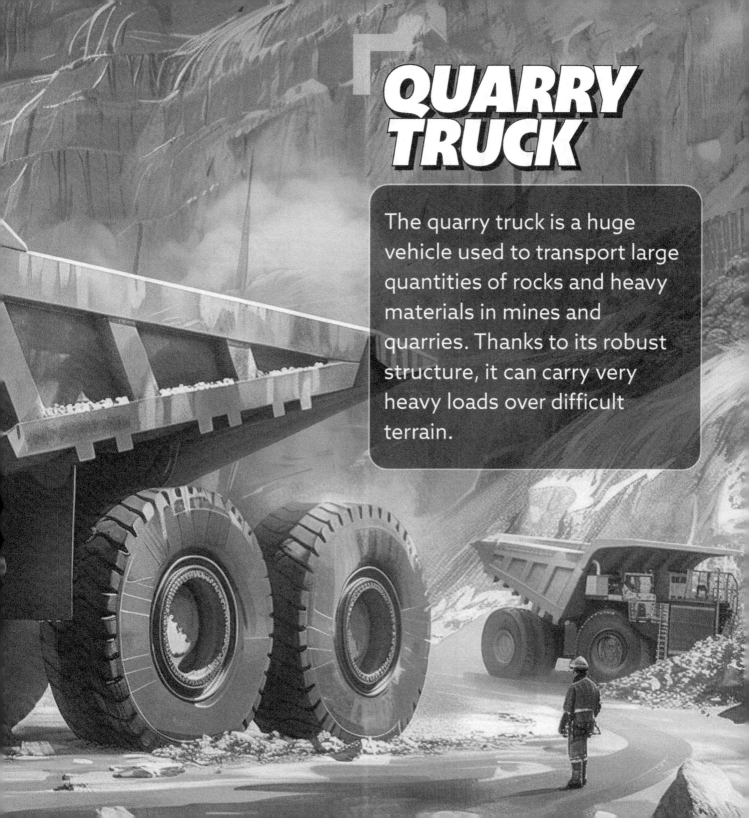

QUARRY TRUCK

The quarry truck is a huge vehicle used to transport large quantities of rocks and heavy materials in mines and quarries. Thanks to its robust structure, it can carry very heavy loads over difficult terrain.

THE IMPORTANCE OF TEAMWORK

DID YOU KNOW?

MANAGING THE TRAFFIC OF HEAVY VEHICLES WITHIN A QUARRY IS VERY IMPORTANT!

In a quarry, there are many heavy vehicles like bulldozers, trucks, and excavators working together.

To avoid accidents and ensure that work proceeds smoothly, it's necessary to coordinate the movements of all vehicles well.

Operators use signals, radios, and pre-set paths to maintain order and safety. This helps protect workers and ensures that materials are transported quickly and efficiently.

Special vehicles are custom-designed and built to meet specific client needs. These vehicles can be customized with special equipment and unique features to perform particular tasks in various construction sectors.

CUSTOM VEHICLES

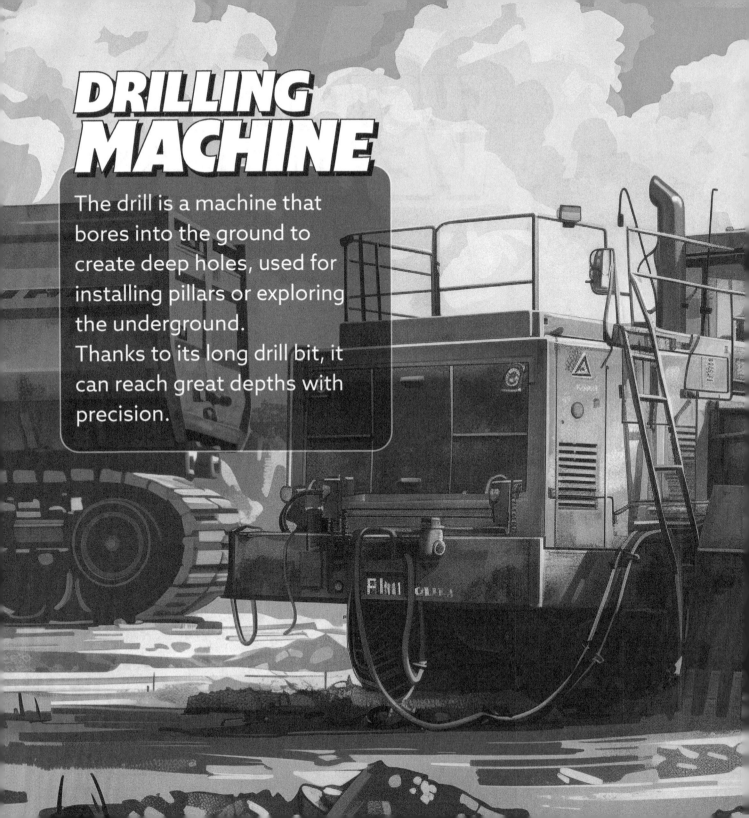

DRILLING MACHINE

The drill is a machine that bores into the ground to create deep holes, used for installing pillars or exploring the underground.
Thanks to its long drill bit, it can reach great depths with precision.

CRANE

The crane is a tall and strong machine that lifts and moves heavy objects on construction sites. Thanks to its long arm and robustness, it is essential for building tall buildings and complex structures.

DID YOU KNOW?

How much can one of the world's most powerful cranes lift?
The world's most powerful crane can lift over 20,000 tons, which is like lifting more than 3,000 elephants!

How does a crane remain stable without falling?
A crane uses heavy counterweights and a wide base to stay stable even when lifting very heavy loads.

What is the maximum height a crane can reach? Some cranes can reach heights over 200 meters, like the large tower cranes used to build skyscrapers.

TELESCOPIC HANDLER

The telescopic handler is a versatile vehicle used to lift loads to great heights. Thanks to its extendable arm, it can reach difficult points and carry heavy materials high up on construction sites.

MOBILE CRANE

The mobile crane is a vehicle that can move and lift heavy loads with its mobile arm. It is essential on construction sites for lifting materials and components that need to be positioned high up.

MISSION: PAVING!

DUMP TRUCK

TANKER TRUCK

STEAMROLLER

BUILDING A NEW ROAD IS TEAMWORK!

Bulldozers level the ground, steamrollers compact the soil to make it solid, and pavers lay the hot asphalt. The steamrollers go over it again to make everything smooth. The dump trucks bring the asphalt to the construction site. All these vehicles work together to make the roads we can drive on!

STEAM ROLLER

The steamroller is used to level and compact the soil or asphalt. It is essential in road construction, making surfaces smooth and hard for safe and smooth traffic.

PAVER

The paver is a machine used to lay asphalt in road construction.
With its feeding and leveling system, it creates a smooth and even road surface, ready to be used by vehicles.

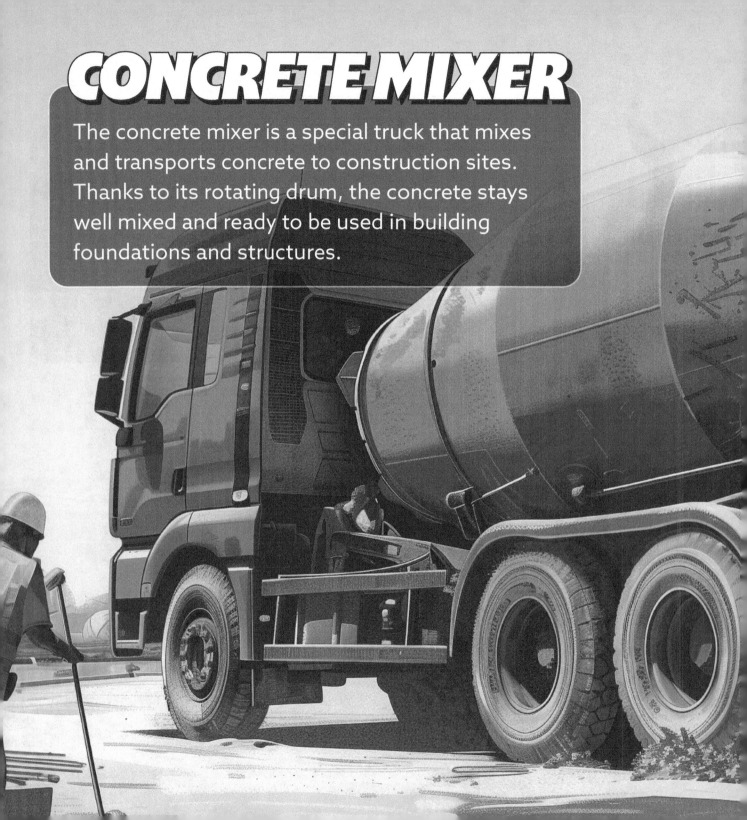

CONCRETE MIXER

The concrete mixer is a special truck that mixes and transports concrete to construction sites. Thanks to its rotating drum, the concrete stays well mixed and ready to be used in building foundations and structures.

ENTRANCE
TUNNEL

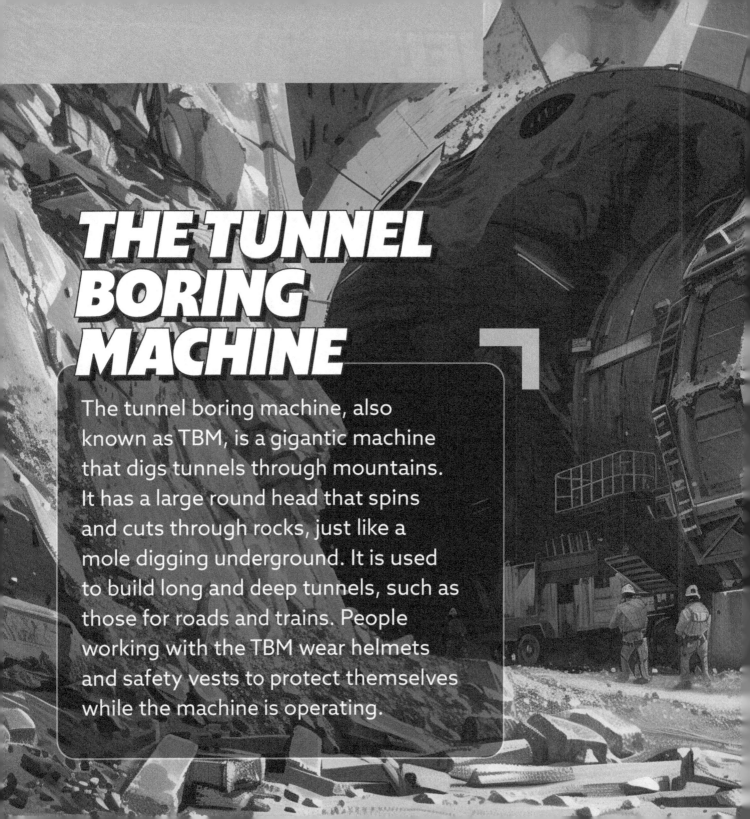

THE TUNNEL BORING MACHINE

The tunnel boring machine, also known as TBM, is a gigantic machine that digs tunnels through mountains. It has a large round head that spins and cuts through rocks, just like a mole digging underground. It is used to build long and deep tunnels, such as those for roads and trains. People working with the TBM wear helmets and safety vests to protect themselves while the machine is operating.

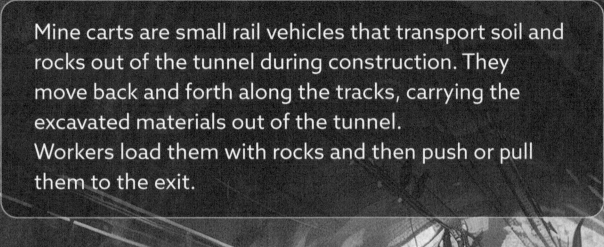

Mine carts are small rail vehicles that transport soil and rocks out of the tunnel during construction. They move back and forth along the tracks, carrying the excavated materials out of the tunnel.
Workers load them with rocks and then push or pull them to the exit.

MINE CARTS

DARKNESS IS NOT A PROBLEM!

Even in the darkest places, such as deep inside a tunnel, work vehicles can do their job thanks to powerful lights and special equipment.

Excavators, drills, and other machinery are equipped with headlights and lighting systems that allow them to work safely, illuminating every corner of the construction site. This way, darkness is never an obstacle to completing important and complex tasks.

DID YOU KNOW?

CAN TUNNELS BE BUILT NOT ONLY THROUGH MOUNTAINS, BUT ALSO UNDERWATER?

Building a tunnel underwater is an incredibly complex job and requires the use of advanced technologies and detailed planning. For example, underwater tunnels are often built using huge machines called tunnel boring machines that dig and line the tunnel as they advance. Additionally, tunnels can be used for roads, railways, and even to transport water and gas from one place to another. Building underwater tunnels helps connect islands, cross rivers, and improve transportation between cities.

THE GREAT MACHINES
OF THE LUMBERJACKS

LOGGING TRUCK

The logging truck is a large vehicle that transports tree logs from the forest to sawmills. It has large sturdy wheels and a very strong frame to carry heavy loads. Workers load the logs onto the truck using special cranes and secure them well for the journey. It is a very important truck to get the wood where it is needed, such as factories and lumber stores.

FORESTRY HARVESTER

The forestry harvester is a powerful machine that works in the woods to cut down trees and turn them into logs. This machinery has a large cutting head that can grab, cut, and delimb trees. It is mounted on sturdy tracks that allow it to move easily over difficult terrain. With its mechanical arm, the harvester can cut down trees and prepare them for transport. It is an essential tool for forestry work, making the job faster and more efficient.

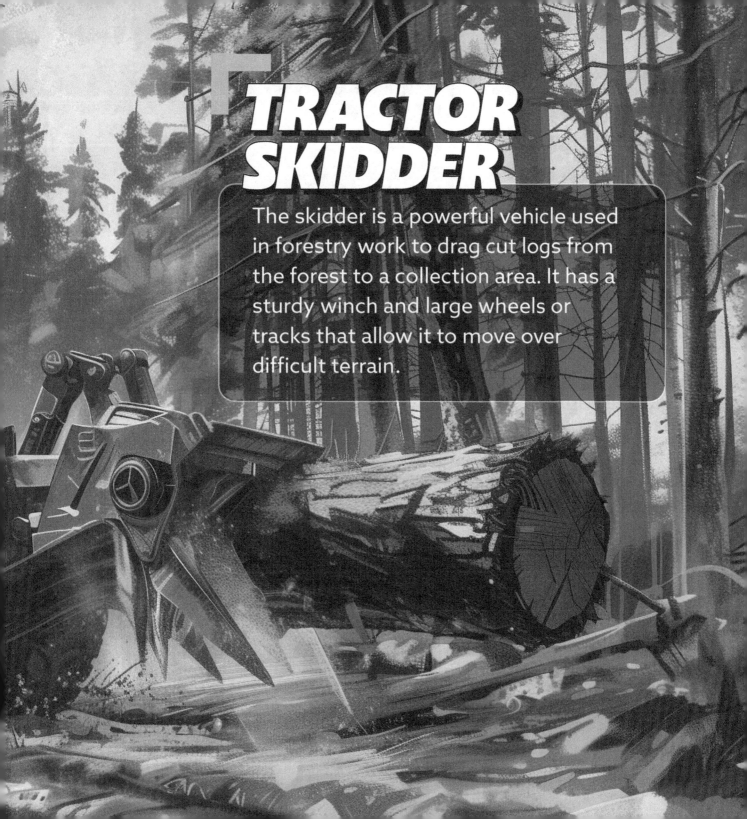

TRACTOR SKIDDER

The skidder is a powerful vehicle used in forestry work to drag cut logs from the forest to a collection area. It has a sturdy winch and large wheels or tracks that allow it to move over difficult terrain.

TO REACH A CUTTING AREA IN THE WOODS, VERY OFTEN YOU FIRST NEED TO BUILD A DIRT ROAD.

These roads allow heavy vehicles to reach the trees to be cut. Once the road is built, the logging collection areas are organized, where the logs are stacked and prepared for transport.

In some cases, cableways are also used to move the logs from hard-to-reach areas directly to the collection areas. Cableways are suspended ropes on which carts travel to transport the wood, making the work faster and safer.

WOOD
DEPOSIT
AREA

DID YOU KNOW?

Or, scan the QR code below and instantly access your Special Content!

SCAN ME

SCANNING

WRO TE.BE CLUB

DOWNLOAD THE BONUS
HERE ARE YOUR SPECIAL CONTENTS

a gift for you

Yes, that's right! We have prepared it just for you.
Getting the special contents is easy.
Follow these steps:

Visit the website: Open your browser and go to the page

wrote.be/en/club

Enter the Code:
You will find a field where you can enter the following exclusive code:

9425E

This code has been created especially for the book owners and will give you access to a bonus with unique resources that you can download directly to your device.

WE NEED YOUR HELP!

In a world where reviews seem to matter most, we need your help more than ever. If you enjoyed this book, please take a few minutes to leave us a review.

Your words are incredibly valuable to us and to help other children discover this fantastic world of construction vehicles.

Imagine the smile on another child's face when they discover these powerful vehicles thanks to your review.

Every single opinion counts and can make a big difference.

We are young creators, and your reviews are the engine that allows us to continue creating and improving.

Thank you so much for y
our time and
support.

Made in the USA
Monee, IL
17 November 2024